A NEW TRADE POLICY TOWARD COMMUNIST COUNTRIES

A Statement on National Policy
by the Research and Policy Committee
of the Committee for Economic Development
September, 1972

Single copy... $1.50

Printed in U.S.A.
First Printing September 1972
Design: Harry Carter
Library of Congress Catalog Card Number: 72-87311
International Standard Book Number: 0-87186-048-1

Committee for Economic Development
477 Madison Avenue, New York, N.Y. 10022

CONTENTS

The Responsibility for
CED Statements on National Policy

This statement has been approved for publication as a statement of the Research and Policy Committee by the members of that Committee, the Subcommittee on East-West Trade, and the International Studies Subcommittee, subject to individual dissents or reservations noted herein. The trustees who are responsible for this statement are listed on pages 5 and 6. Company associates are included for identification only; the companies do not share in the responsibility borne by the individuals.

The Research and Policy Committee is directed by CED's bylaws to:

"Initiate studies into the principles of business policy and of public policy which will foster the full contribution by industry and commerce to the attainment and maintenance of high and secure standards of living for people in all walks of life through maximum employment and high productivity in the domestic economy."

The bylaws emphasize that:

"All research is to be thoroughly objective in character, and the approach in each instance is to be from the standpoint of the general welfare and not from that of any special political or economic group."

The Research and Policy Committee is composed of 60 Trustees from among the 200 businessmen and educators who comprise the Committee for Economic Development. It is aided by a Research Advisory Board of leading economists, a small permanent Research Staff, and by advisors chosen for their competence in the field being considered.

Each Statement on National Policy is preceded by discussions, meetings, and exchanges of memoranda, often stretching over many months. The research is undertaken by a subcommittee, with its advisors, and the full Research and Policy Committee participates in the drafting of findings and recommendations.

Except for the members of the Research and Policy Committee and the responsible subcommittee, the recommendations presented herein are not necessarily endorsed by other Trustees or by the advisors, contributors, staff members, or others associated with CED.

The Research and Policy Committee offers these Statements on National Policy as an aid to clearer understanding of the steps to be taken in achieving sustained growth of the American economy. The Committee is not attempting to pass on any pending specific legislative proposals; its purpose is to urge careful consideration of the objectives set forth in the statement and of the best means of accomplishing those objectives.

4.

5.

6.

FOREWORD

For some time there has been growing recognition in the United States that economic and political advantages would ensue from modifying the special restrictions that have substantially reduced U.S. trade with the communist countries for more than twenty years. By 1970 the Administration began to remove some of these obstacles to East-West trade on a step-by-step basis, a process which was accelerated in 1972 by the President's visits to Peking and Moscow.

In this statement, which was undertaken as a sequel to CED's 1965 policy statement on *East-West Trade: A Common Policy for the West,* the Research and Policy Committee gives substantial support to this shift in U.S. policy. The Committee bases its position in part on the ground that trading partners tend to achieve mutually beneficial economic gains and thus develop a greater stake in settling political disputes peacefully. But the statement carefully avoids any suggestion that problems will not still face the companies and governments of the Western market-oriented economies in doing business with the centrally planned, state-trading countries of the East. Notwithstanding these difficulties, however, the six members of the European Community increased their combined trade with the Eastern countries by roughly 280 per cent from 1960 to 1970, while U.S. trade with the East rose by only 60 per cent. Moreover, in their economic relations with the East—especially the Soviet Union—Western Europe and Japan have moved beyond export and import trade to coproduction agreements involving investments in joint production of industrial products as well as joint development of raw materials.

A major issue that still faces the United States and other Western countries is how, and to what extent, rules for East-West economic relations can be developed through international organizations. The issue was discussed several times at meetings with CED's counterpart organizations in Britain, France, Germany, Japan, and Sweden. This led to a brief joint statement, "Multilateral Policies for East-West Trade and Payments," which follows Chapter III of this document.

Discussions with the other organizations, and our own research and deliberations, were carried out for CED by the Panel on East-West Trade and the International Studies Subcommittee. The Research and Policy Committee is deeply indebted to all members of the panel which prepared the statement, especially to Chairman William H. Franklin, as well as to the advisors of the panel and the subcommittee. Roy Blough of Columbia University, the Project Director, deserves special recognition for his contribution to the background research and drafting of the statement.

We express our gratitude to The Ford Foundation for its financial support of this study on East-West Trade.

PHILIP M. KLUTZNICK, *Chairman*
Research and Policy Committee

The joint statement, MULTILATERAL POLICIES FOR EAST-WEST TRADE AND PAYMENTS, on pages 37-44 of this document, has been adopted by the British, French, German, and Japanese organizations as well as by CED, and is being released by them in their own countries.

The Swedish organization participated in the preparation of the joint statement but, in accordance with its rules, will distribute it as a study rather than issuing it as a policy statement.

I.

INTRODUCTION

■ The Research and Policy Committee has consistently supported the U.S. government's policy of moving toward a progressively liberalized international trade and payments system. The Committee's support for this policy has been based on a belief that the expansion of international trade will promote the economic, political, and security interests of the United States.

In line with this position we applaud the steps taken in recent months by the Administration to reduce the special prohibitions and other obstacles that the United States has placed in the way of trade with communist countries for more than two decades. We also favor further removal of such restrictions. At the same time, we recognize that there will be some apprehension at the prospect of moving rapidly in opening the door to trade with countries whose international political objectives, economic systems, and trading methods differ so much from our own.*

---

*See Memorandum by MR. MARVIN BOWER, page 45.

Against this background, and in support of our recommendations, we:

First, explain our reasons for believing that there should be greater freedom of trade between the United States and the centrally planned, state-trading countries.

Second, explore the problems involved in achieving this increased trade with maximum benefit and minimum damage to U.S. national interests and to the international economic and political order.

Third, appraise current developments in U.S. economic relations with state-trading or "Eastern" countries and the prospects for continued growth of trade and other mutually beneficial economic arrangements with them.

We believe that as a matter of principle special constraints should not be imposed on the functioning of international markets except as required by an overriding public interest, and that if such constraints are imposed they should be removed as the public interest permits. The practical values to be served by removing restrictions on international trade include economic benefits but extend well beyond them. At a time when the United States and the state-trading socialist countries have been seeking ways to improve and stabilize their mutual political relationships, willingness to trade is in itself a sign of amity that helps dissipate tensions. Through trade, moreover, new channels of communication are opened which help reduce the danger of either side misinterpreting the intentions of the other. Trading partners tend to have an increased stake in the peaceful settlement of disputes. Although improved communication and mutual understanding cannot be expected to solve fundamental conflicts of interest, they at least encourage a rational approach to negotiating a maximum area of agreement—as indicated by President Nixon's discussions in Moscow during May 1972 and the subsequent trade negotiations between the United States and the Soviet Union.

Another source of benefit from interchange and cooperation with communist countries is in the area of scientific research and technology. In medicine and public health, in nuclear fusion as a source of energy, in space technology, and in other areas, the exchange of ideas and closer cooperation could yield mutual benefits.

The potential benefits of increasing East-West trade by the removal of special restrictions are too promising to be neglected.* This would be true even if there were no desire to develop closer political and cultural relations with the state-trading countries. Larger international

---

*See Memorandum by MR. STEWART S. CORT, page 45.

markets open to each nation make possible more trade and investment. This, in turn, increases the mutually beneficial economic gains to be realized from industrial specialization and exchange. Over the past two decades, of course, the volume of trade between the United States and the communist countries has been too small to permit realization of the potential economic, political, and security benefits.*

Chapter II of this policy statement deals with past and potential trade between the state-trading countries and the market economies of the West. In Chapter III, this Committee considers the special restrictions that the United States has imposed on its trade with the Eastern countries, proposes that these restrictions be substantially reduced, and indicates the need for multilateral rules and regulations to harmonize national policies of the Western countries in their trade with the East. A separate statement follows which presents the joint views of this Committee and of CED's counterpart organizations in Japan and Western Europe with respect to multilateral arrangements for East-West trade.

In this document, for purposes of convenience, the centrally planned, state-trading socialist countries are also referred to as communist countries, Eastern countries, or the East, while the market-oriented Western economies are referred to as Western countries, or the West.

---

*See Memorandum by MR. PHILIP SPORN, page 46.

UNITED STATES TRADE WITH COMMUNIST COUNTRIES: PAST AND POTENTIAL

■ The communist countries in 1970 participated in about one-tenth of the world's export and import trade. Slightly more than three-fifths of the communist country trade was with other communist countries, one-fourth with Western industrial countries, and the remainder with developing countries.[1] The following are a few of the more significant generalizations which statistics disclose:

1. United States trade with the communist countries has been relatively very small, accounting for less than 1 per cent of their trade as well as of U.S. trade.

2. Trade with the East of most other Western industrialized countries, though a small proportion of their total trade, was relatively much greater than that of the United States. For example, in 1971, the trade of the six European Community (EC) members with the East (which included exports of U.S. manufacturing subsidiaries operating in the Community) was more than ten times as great as that of the United States, and the trade of the European Free Trade Area (EFTA) was almost six times larger.

3. During the decade 1960-1970, Eastern trade—both with the developing countries and with the industrial countries of the West—

---

[1]/For the trade of the United States and the other principal Western countries with the East, see page 13 and the Appendix.

TRADE OF OECD COUNTRIES WITH COMMUNIST COUNTRIES, 1971

(millions of U.S. dollars, f.o.b. and c.i.f.*)

OECD Country or Area	Exports to:		Imports from:	
	World	Communist Countries	World	Communist Countries
EC total	100,819[a]	3,794[b]	99,352[c]	3,532[b]
EFTA total	48,414[d]	2,230	55,834[e]	2,711
U.S.A.	44,137	384	45,602	228
Japan	24,010	1,147	19,715	944
Canada	17,676	379	15,460	102
Other OECD	5,222	214	9,510	297

**Exports are f.o.b.; imports are f.o.b. for U.S.A. and Canada, and c.i.f. for European countries and Japan.*
[a]/*Includes $49,639 million of exports to other EC countries.*
[b]/*Excludes trade between West Germany and East Germany. Estimates for 1970 put West Germany's exports to East Germany at $660.0 million (f.o.b.) and its imports at $545.6 million (c.i.f.).*
[c]/*Includes $49,583 million of imports from other EC countries.*
[d]/*Includes $13,552 million of exports to other EFTA countries.*
[e]/*Includes $14,141 million of imports from other EFTA countries.*
Source: OECD, *Statistics of Foreign Trade,* Series A (April 1972).

U.S. TRADE WITH COMMUNIST COUNTRIES, 1971

(millions of U.S. dollars, f.o.b.)

U.S. Trade with	Exports to:	Imports from:	Balance[a]
World	**44,137**	**45,602**	**−1,465**
Sino-Soviet Bloc, total	**384**	**228**	**+ 156**
U.S.S.R.	162	58	+ 104
East Germany	25	10	+ 15
Poland	73	107	− 34
Czechoslovakia	39	24	+ 15
Hungary	28	8	+ 20
Romania	53	14	+ 39
Bulgaria	4	3	+ 1
China	***	5	− 5
Other	***	***	***

[a]/ *(+) = excess of exports, (−) = excess of imports.*
****Less than $500,000.*
Source: OECD, *Statistics of Foreign Trade,* Series A (April 1972).

increased by somewhat larger percentages than did total world trade, nearly tripling in dollar volume. Over the decade, however, the communist countries shifted their trade to some extent away from other Eastern countries to the industrial West, and also reduced bilateral balancing on a country-by-country basis.

4. Between 1960 and 1970 the combined exports of the Western industrial countries to the East consisted of less than one-fifth primary products (mainly food) while manufactures (primarily engineering products, chemicals, and iron and steel) accounted for some four-fifths of the total. In contrast, a little more than half of their imports from the East consisted of primary products, mainly food.

FACTORS AFFECTING THE TRADE POTENTIAL

Undoubtedly the small U.S. share of Western trade with communist countries has been due in large part to the special governmental restrictions imposed by the United States on its trade with the East.* To some extent it has also been due in recent years to our lack of competitiveness in certain products. Removing the special U.S. restrictions, however, would not necessarily lead to a rapid expansion of trade with the communist countries. Other factors will continue to limit our trade with the Eastern countries, including their economic institutions and trading policies, as well as continued competition from other Western countries.

It will clearly take time for the United States to overcome the advantages of the other noncommunist countries that have established contacts and relationships in Eastern Europe and the U.S.S.R. as well as in China. However, the most important factor affecting the U.S. trade potential in Eastern countries may well be the extent to which there is complementarity between the U.S. economy and the communist economies—taking into account not only comparative advantages in production but also geographical location and costs of transportation.**

Economic Factors Underlying Trade Potential

Removal or reduction of U.S. trade restrictions undoubtedly would result in some increase in the amount and variety of trade with the communist countries. The end of the embargo on exports to China opens a door to two-way trade that has been entirely closed. In the more relaxed political climate, U.S. businessmen can be expected to be more aggressive in marketing in the U.S.S.R. and Eastern Europe, while elim-

*See Memorandum by MR. HERMAN L. WEISS, page 46.
**See Memorandum by MR. STEWART S. CORT, page 47.

ination of our differentially high tariffs will encourage U.S. purchases from these countries and in turn make it easier for them to finance imports from the United States.*

With the removal or reduction of U.S. restrictions, the growth of trade will be determined more than in the past by economic and business considerations. Some of these are favorable. For example, U.S. machinery exports to Eastern Europe and the U.S.S.R. can be expected to increase, perhaps substantially. In general, however, no great or sudden increase in trade should be expected. For one thing, the total volume of communist trade, including trade among communist countries, is small relative to population and national income.

The diversity of resources and the size of populations in countries as large as the U.S.S.R. and China enable them to develop a wide variety of industries. Thus, they have less need than smaller countries to trade across their borders, a factor which has been reinforced by policies of economic self-containment and independence. Such policies were faithfully pursued in the U.S.S.R. from the early 1920's to the 1950's and appear to be strong in China today. In addition, the Soviet Union still prefers to trade with the socialist countries of Eastern Europe.

Another deterrent to U.S. trade with the East is that for the near future the growth of U.S. exports to communist countries is likely to be largely dependent on our imports from them and the credits we grant, rather than on the development of multilateral trade involving other Western countries. The communist countries are in a position to supply the United States with raw materials and low-technology goods (such as semifinished products, shoes, ceramics, and glass) as well as some industrial equipment. The United States, however, is not eager to add new suppliers of low-technology manufactures since it already has political as well as economic problems in adjusting its industrial structure to absorb an increasing volume of such goods from existing suppliers. Moreover, the developing noncommunist countries have a broad commitment from the U.S. Administration to get congressional approval of tariff preferences for imports of their manufactures.

However, a new aspect of U.S. economic relations with the East is beginning to emerge. Some U.S. companies are now considering whether it may be possible to make satisfactory arrangements with Moscow for cooperative ventures to develop certain fuels and minerals in the Soviet Union. There is a possibility that similar arrangements might eventually be made with China. Both countries have large unexploited

---

*See Memorandum by MR. STEWART S. CORT, page 47.

15.

supplies of these resources which will require vast amounts of capital, technology, and managerial know-how for their development. Such cooperative ventures* would involve coproduction arrangements in which U.S. business firms could provide the capital, technology, and management needed, while receiving payment in the product over a considerable number of years. Coproduction arrangements have been made between Japan and the U.S.S.R. for developing the resources of Siberia, and others are being considered. It is another matter whether, in terms of the heavy investment and other commitments required, the prospective value of the product received would be found sufficiently attractive for U.S. companies to get substantially involved in such agreements.**

As for U.S. exports, the prospects probably are best for increasing sales of certain types of heavy machinery, plant, and advanced technology which the communist countries need and the United States is in a favorable position to supply. In addition, the Soviet Union, which has imported U.S. wheat for some years, may also become a continuing market for corn and oilseeds not grown in adequate quantities there. China, which also is importing wheat (principally from Canada), may want to buy U.S. wheat in the future since we have a wider range of qualities better adapted to Chinese requirements than does Canada.

In the case of manufactured consumer goods, the communist countries are not likely to become important markets for U.S. exports in the near future. For one thing, these countries at their present levels of development prefer to save their foreign exchange to buy industrial equipment and other requirements for rapid development. Moreover, for many types of consumer goods the United States is not competitive with the existing suppliers in Western Europe, Japan, and Southeast Asia.[2]*** Such low-cost production centers as Hong Kong may well step up their efforts to sell consumer goods to the communist countries in order to make up for sales lost due to restrictions placed on their exports of such goods to the United States and Western Europe.

It would be premature to try to estimate the probable rate of growth of U.S. trade with communist countries, including the two-way trade that could result from investment through coproduction arrangements. Whatever the potentialities, their realization is dependent on (1)

[2]/The lack of competitiveness is partly a matter of production costs but also involves nearness to the market, transport costs, speed of delivery, credit terms, and adaptation of products to local needs and tastes.

*See Memorandum by MR. GAYLORD FREEMAN, page 47.
**See Memorandum by MR. STEWART S. CORT, page 47.
***See Memorandum by MR. HERMAN L. WEISS, page 47.

16.

continued reduction of U.S. restrictions on trade with the East,* and (2) willingness of the communist countries to increase their trade with the United States.**

Government Restrictions

During most of the quarter century since World War II, the United States imposed an embargo on trade with China and North Korea—an embargo which was then extended to Cuba and North Vietnam. In the case of other communist countries, the United States limited the types of products that could be exported, imposed differentially high tariffs on imports, denied government credit guarantees (as well as limiting the scope of private credit), and in other ways restricted trade with the East. These restrictions are described in Chapter III.

Some of the impact of U.S. barriers to trade with communist countries can be attributed to competition of other Western countries which imposed fewer restrictions on trade with the East and granted more liberal credit terms.

It is more difficult to judge to what extent the centrally planned, state-trading system of the communist countries has held down the volume of trade with the United States. We can only infer indirectly what the effects of the Eastern system have been, since it is applied through the unpublicized buying or selling decisions of the state-trading monopolies rather than through publicly known laws and rules applied to private business firms.

This state-trading system is linked closely with the policy of economic autarky which was dominant in the U.S.S.R. until after the death of Stalin in 1953. Under a policy of economic autarky, trade is held to the minimum necessary to import the instruments of economic development needed to make the country self-sufficient. In recent years, however, the Soviet Union has sought to import Western machinery, plants, and technology, preferably on liberal credit terms. Some observers view this development as no more than a temporary effort to achieve self-sufficiency at a higher level. Others believe there is growing recognition in the U.S.S.R. of the longer-run economic advantages of expanded trade with Western industrial nations.***

With respect to the state-trading countries of Eastern Europe, autarky is a serious disadvantage since they cannot hope to become self-

*See Memorandum by MR. GAYLORD FREEMAN, page 48.
**See Memoranda by MR. PHILIP SPORN, and by MR. HERMAN L. WEISS, page 48.
***See Memorandum by MR. PHILIP SPORN, page 48.

17.

sufficient. The U.S.S.R. continues to contain the trade of these countries to the greatest extent possible within the COMECON[3] organization which it initiated and largely dominates. However, most of the other COMECON members have been eager to increase their trade with the Western countries not only to gain purely economic benefits but also to reduce Soviet domination of their economies.

China, since its break with the U.S.S.R., has been increasing its trade with the West. This trend can be expected to increase as a result of China's renewed economic growth and its desire to promote industrialization and greater economic self-sufficiency. A key question is how much the United States will get of this increased trade, in view of U.S. relationships with China since the communists took control in the late 1940's.

Attitude of the U.S. Public to Expanded Communist Trade

In the past, public opinion in the United States has supported the restrictions imposed by the government on trade with communist countries. Now the public appears to be supporting the relaxation of those restrictions. It would be difficult to demonstrate which, over the years, has been more important: the influence of public opinion in shaping governmental policy toward East-West trade, or the reverse.*Obviously there has been an interaction of the two.

In any case, it is clear that members of the American public can place obstacles in the way of expanded trade with the communist countries if the policy of relaxation is not generally accepted, or if there is a turn for the worse in political relations. At times in the past, private groups have sponsored consumer boycotts, municipal ordinances have forbidden the sale of communist products, and workers have refused to handle goods bound for or coming from communist countries. The leaders of labor unions have recently expressed opposition to increasing imports from the East. Some business executives refused in the 1960's even to consider closer business relations with the state-trading countries because of concern that consumers or workers would raise difficulties for their companies.

Such public reactions to trade with the communist countries are undesirable for at least three reasons: first, the apprehensions widely accepted in the past no longer appear to be justified; second, the main-

---

[3]/The Council for Mutual Economic Assistance is an economic organization of the centrally planned economies of Eastern Europe (Bulgaria, Czechoslovakia, East Germany, Hungary, Poland, Romania), the U.S.S.R., and the Mongolian People's Republic.

*See Memorandum by MR. PHILIP SPORN, page 49.

tenance of restrictions by the United States is a gesture in futility since other trading nations have relaxed their restrictions; and third, the rules of international trade are better left to the federal government and not carried on through coercive actions by private organizations or by state and local governments. There is urgent need for better public understanding of the contribution that improved trading relations can make to the achievement and maintenance of world peace.

Communist Institutions and Practices

The economic institutions and practices of the communist countries inevitably create special trading difficulties for the business firms and governments of the market-oriented economies. Despite these difficulties, the experience of Western Europe and Japan over the past ten years shows that trade can be carried on profitably with the communist countries. The problems, however, are sufficiently important to require consideration. They arise from a combination of policies, the major ones being central planning, state-trading monopolies, and bilateral trade and payments agreements. All exist, of course, within the framework of government ownership of the means of production.

Central planning in communist countries relies predominantly on administrative decisions on what to produce, how to allocate resources, and how to determine prices, wages, taxes, government services, etc. The decisions of the planners are designed to promote the government's objectives, which may diverge widely from consumer wants.

The Eastern countries generally prefer to meet virtually all their basic needs from domestic production. Accordingly, the composition and volume of foreign trade are prescribed in the central plan after decisions are made on planning domestic production. At times communist trade has been used to dispose of unplanned surpluses or to meet unplanned shortages, with resulting discontinuities that discourage foreign trading partners. It is not surprising that the development of sophisticated marketing techniques has been neglected in such a system.

In centrally planned production and resource allocation there is no necessary link between economic costs and prices. Thus, it is difficult to apply the usual criteria to ascertain whether foreign trade is subsidized. Furthermore, there is little or no basis for determining whether or not any given foreign exchange rate is close to an "equilibrium" value.

In communist countries, trade in each category of goods is made the responsibility of one of about a score of state-trading organizations which is given the monopoly of importing and exporting goods in that category. These trading monopolies are distinct and separate from the state enterprises that produce the goods for export and that seek to have goods imported. The separation has prevented most foreign producers from carrying on direct negotiations or even having direct contact with the final users. Similarly, it has prevented foreign buyers from having such contacts with producers. By limiting the importing or exporting function for any one product to a single organization, the communist country maximizes its bargaining position relative to prospective trading partners and competitors. Of course this bargaining strength is offset in many instances by the superior access a large foreign supplier or customer may have to world markets and sources of supply.

Bilateral trading and payments agreements are the dominant and preferred method of carrying on trade in the communist world. Bilateral trading agreements serve the purposes of central planning by being much easier to manage than would be multilateral trade. They fit well into a system of state-trading monopolies, and do not require the country to have a convertible currency or realistic foreign exchange rates in order to carry on trade.

Some of the problems encountered by U.S. companies in negotiating business transactions in communist countries are also met in many other countries, especially the less developed ones, and thus have no necessary connection with communism. Other problems do have such a connection. Foreign competitors of U.S. companies are given a preference if they are from Western countries that have bilateral trading agreements with communist countries, as are suppliers from other communist countries. An attractive bid by U.S. exporters or importers may be disqualified in an Eastern country by an unexplained veto that is based on national policy considerations. Business prospects are difficult to assess where arbitrary costing and pricing criteria provide no basis for judgment as to needs or supplies. However badly the product may be needed in such a country, it must be called for in the economic plan if it is to be purchased.

State-trading monopolies have sometimes insisted on tied transactions and compensatory deals that require a Western company to engage in the marketing of products which it may not want. The trading monopoly may try to use its bargaining power to insist upon unusual contract terms on a take-it-or-leave-it basis. In third markets, or even in his domestic market, the noncommunist producer may have to compete with a communist trading corporation which does not need to cover cost and may not even know what the cost was to the communist producer. Nor do Western firms, as a rule, get permission from Eastern governments to establish representative offices, hire local help, do on-the-spot maintenance of equipment, or make use of other usually available facilities.

Collection of royalties for the licensing of know-how is frequently impractical in some communist countries, for example, the U.S.S.R. This is because of the inability to secure detailed, or even reliable, information on the volume of production, sales, or profits. The protection of trademarks and copyrights is not adequate in Western terms, although the earlier lack of patent protection has been remedied. In general, the unusual provisions of communist law and the practices of People's Courts may cause apprehension, thus discouraging Western businessmen.*

These and other difficulties have undoubtedly restricted the volume of U.S. trade with communist countries. Recent developments, however, are encouraging. The United Nations Economic Commission for Europe (ECE) has been vigorously sponsoring a dialogue on East-West trade problems and promoting improvements in the protection of industrial property, in commercial arbitration, etc. In these respects there has been some progress by Eastern European countries in conforming to Western practices, and to a lesser extent by the U.S.S.R.**

On the governmental side, however, communist institutions and practices still prevent Eastern countries from fitting into the international system developed by the industrialized Western countries to promote nondiscriminatory multilateral trade and payments. For example, the communist countries are not members of the International Monetary Fund (IMF) and their currencies are inconvertible.

Perhaps most troublesome is the impossibility of applying the basic rules of the General Agreement on Tariffs and Trade (GATT) to trade with the communist countries. Rules designed to prevent the discriminations and distortion of trade that may be caused by tariffs, quotas, subsidies, and dumping are meaningless for the state-trading monopolies.*** Their decisions regarding prices as well as preferences among customers or suppliers can frustrate all the GATT rules. Despite the formal GATT proscription of political discrimination, moreover, the state-trading monopolies are under no effective constraints against using trade as a political weapon. They can do this by discriminating among companies and countries in granting or withholding advantageous trade.

---

*See Memorandum by MR. HERMAN L. WEISS, page 50.
**See Memorandum by MR. PHILIP SPORN, page 50.
***See Memorandum by MR. STEWART S. CORT, page 51.

III.

REDUCING UNITED STATES RESTRICTIONS ON EAST-WEST TRADE

■ For more than two decades the United States has had two distinct policies for world trade: a liberal one for trade with noncommunist countries and a very restrictive one for trade with communist countries. Until recently the United States has been the international leader in promoting both of these trading regimes. The restrictive U.S. policies toward the communist countries date back to the late 1940's.

Until near the end of the 1960's there were only minor changes in our East-West trade policy, except for Yugoslavia and to a lesser degree Poland and Romania. As political relations between the United States and the Eastern countries improved, a number of liberalizing changes were made in U.S. policy especially after 1969. Further policy changes can now be anticipated.

RESTRICTIONS ON EXPORTS

The major U.S. restrictions on trade with the East have been on exports. Their purpose was to prevent communist countries from acquiring goods and technologies that would strengthen their industrial capacity, particularly in the military area. Export controls against particular communist countries were initiated in reaction to the Cold War, the Berlin Blockade, the communist revolution in China, the Korean War, the Castro take-over in Cuba, and the war in Vietnam.

The Export Controls and Embargo

The principal legislation authorizing export controls was the Export Control Act of 1949. This was periodically extended until it was succeeded by the somewhat liberalized Export Administration Act of 1969, which in turn has been extended pending possible revisions. The entry of the Chinese into the Korean War in 1950 was the occasion for the President to make use of the powers conferred by the Trading with the Enemy Act of 1917, which had never been repealed. An embargo on all trade and other transactions with China and North Korea was imposed and this included transactions of the foreign subsidiaries of U.S. corporations. The embargo was subsequently extended to Cuba after the widespread expropriation of foreign property there, and to North Vietnam in connection with the hostilities in Indochina.

Under both the Export Control Act and the Export Administration Act, the President has had virtually complete discretionary authority to impose restrictions on exports from the United States, except for taxing exports which is forbidden by the Constitution (Article I). All exports were placed under license except in the case of Canada. Goods that could be exported freely were put under general license, while those not on this list required a special license.

The countries of the world were divided into several groups, depending on the degree of restriction intended. In operation, the restrictions were applied almost entirely to exports going either directly or indirectly to communist countries. Exports to all these countries were subject to some restrictions, but restrictions varied depending on the country to which the goods were destined.[1] In general, the prohibited

---

[1]The degree of restriction depended on an administrative judgment of the probability and degree of danger to U.S. national security from the export. In these groupings a virtual embargo was applied on exports to North Korea, North Vietnam, Cuba, and, until recently, China. The restrictions on exports to China and the Soviet Union con-

exports to the East included all munitions and other military supplies plus machinery and technology that could be used to produce them.

To make the export restrictions effective, it was obviously necessary to get the cooperation of other Western industrial countries. At the initiative of the United States, the NATO[2] countries plus Japan established the Coordinating Committee on Export Controls (COCOM) in 1950. This organization established a list of the commodities and technologies that were not to be exported to the East. During the Korean War many countries joined the United States in establishing the more restrictive China Committee (CHINCOM) list, which applied to trade with China and North Korea. After the Korean War, however, there was a gradual erosion of support for CHINCOM, and eventually the U.S. differential against China was abandoned by many COCOM countries.[3]

The impact of U.S. restrictions on East-West trade was accentuated by time-consuming administrative procedures with which it was difficult to comply. There were also restrictions on travel, which were a counterpart of those U.S. businessmen met in the communist countries.

Liberalization of Export Controls Since 1969

The major moves by the United States to liberalize export controls began in 1969. Even before then the number of items on the COCOM list had been decreased under pressure from the cooperating governments. They insisted on reducing the list in the light of changing technological and economic developments in the different communist countries.[4]

The way was paved for liberalization of restrictions on U.S. trade with communist countries by a succession of official governmental com-

---

tinue to be greater than on exports to the Eastern European countries. Even among these countries distinctions are made—for example, lesser restrictions are placed on exports to Poland and Romania than to other members of the Warsaw Pact, while Yugoslavia is treated much as are Western countries. The United States does not grant a license in case the final destination of the goods is a prohibited country, regardless of the location of the immediate consignee and whether the shipment is of materials, components, finished goods, or technology.

2/North Atlantic Treaty Organization.

3/Under the Foreign Asset Control Regulations applying the Trading with the Enemy Act, persons subject to the jurisdiction of the United States are still forbidden to engage in any unlicensed financial or commercial transaction with North Korea, North Vietnam, or Cuba. The embargo on trade with these countries has been virtually complete and this was the case also with China, which was indeed the principal target, until the embargo on trade with China was lifted by President Nixon in 1971. In the case of Cuba, the Organization of American States did agree to the embargo at the urging of the United States, although not all Latin American countries are participating in it and it appears to be losing support in Latin America.

4/The U.S. list of items was always longer than the COCOM list, since the Europeans were not willing to be as restrictive as the United States.

mittee reports beginning at about the time CED's 1965 statement on *East-West Trade*[5] was published. In 1969, extensive congressional hearings were held, during which stress was put on the desirability of relaxing U.S. restrictions. For the first time since the beginning of the Cold War the Congress urged the expansion of East-West trade, while backing continued Presidential authority to control such trade. Some adjustments were then made in the administration of the controls to make their impact more predictable and to simplify compliance with them.

The President initiated a separate series of steps on trading with the People's Republic of China, moving away from the virtual prohibition of exports and all economic transactions. He successively lifted the ban on tourist purchases, the importation of art objects by museums, and the embargo on trade with China by foreign subsidiaries of U.S. companies. In 1971 the embargo was lifted on trading with China by U.S. companies themselves. In February 1972 the list of restricted items was made the same as that for the U.S.S.R.

Little change was noticeable in trade with the U.S.S.R. until 1971. Sales of wheat to Moscow during the Kennedy Administration led to considerable public criticism and also resulted in a successful demand by the maritime unions that 50 per cent of exports to communist countries must go in U.S. bottoms. The resultant higher shipping costs ended the sales of wheat and discouraged other trade, which led President Nixon to remove the 50 per cent requirement in the autumn of 1971. Approval was given by the Department of Commerce for U.S. companies to bid on the construction of a truck foundry in the Soviet Union.

In February 1972, the President removed the special restrictions that had been imposed on the exports of foreign subsidiaries of U.S. companies. His action placed these subsidiaries on the same basis, so far as U.S. controls were concerned, as foreign companies subject to the laws and policy of the country in which they were operating. This action was a particularly welcome one both to foreign governments, which considered the restrictions an improper intrusion on their sovereignty, and to these U.S. parent firms which had been caught up in the intergovernmental jurisdictional dispute. There has also been a streamlining of U.S. procedures and a cooperative approach toward mutual reduction in visa and travel restrictions. The communist countries, for their part, have taken a more favorable position on trade with the United States. The

[5]*East-West Trade: A Common Policy for the West,* A Statement on National Policy by the Research and Policy Committee, Committee for Economic Development (New York: May 1965).

Eastern European members of COMECON have no reluctance about trading with this country except as they may be discouraged by Soviet policy.

The Soviet Union itself has begun to show more interest in trade with the United States. This was demonstrated at the May 1972 summit meeting in Moscow during which President Nixon held lengthy discussions with Soviet leaders on expanding trade between the United States and the U.S.S.R. Preliminary discussions had already been held by the U.S. Secretary of Commerce who headed a mission to Moscow in late 1971 and reported optimistically on the prospects for enlarged trade between the United States and the Soviet Union.

According to this report, Soviet officials indicated (1) the U.S.S.R. desire to buy plants and technology; (2) the importance of receiving most-favored-nation (MFN) treatment on exports to the United States; (3) the Soviet need for credit; and (4) their desire for U.S. firms to join in coproduction arrangements to develop Soviet natural resources.*

The attitude of China toward doing business with the United States appears to be fluid. However, during the President's visit to China late in February 1972, an understanding was reached that the door to trade should be opened on a bilateral basis. Preliminary steps in this direction have been taken. For example, some U.S. business firms attended the Canton Fair during April and May 1972, and several reported making direct purchases of Chinese goods.

The U.S. export control program, covering the U.S.S.R., Eastern Europe, and China, now includes only the COCOM list, in which other Western countries join, and a number of additional items on the U.S. restricted list. There has been no change in the restrictions and embargo on North Korea, North Vietnam, or Cuba. Even excluding these countries from consideration, however, the export control chapter of U.S. history should not be treated as closed. There continues to be considerable opposition in the United States to the resumption of normal trading relations with communist countries.

Maintaining Export Restrictions on East-West Trade

As a result of the U.S. controls, American business firms and their foreign subsidiaries** have been deprived of numerous export opportunities. These have been seized by European and Japanese business competitors, who were not excluded from trade with China, were subject to

---

*See Memorandum by MR. STEWART S. CORT, page 51.
**See Memorandum by MR. HERMAN L. WEISS, page 51.

26.

the shorter COCOM list, and were restrained—many U.S. businessmen believe—by less rigorous administration and far fewer delaying procedures. The more restrictive policy of the United States failed in its objectives to the extent that other nations supplied what the United States withheld. For many, this in itself is sufficient reason for the United States to abandon the policy and get its share of the market—to the advantage not only of U.S. business firms, but also labor, the government, investors, and the public generally.

Looking to the future, it is important to assess how and to what extent the restriction of exports to communist countries advances the national security of the United States. Withholding supplies of goods necessary to fight a war is most effective during a "hot" war or when the threat of war is imminent. The losses to the United States, and to the friendly countries it desires to support, are then deemed to be less important than the deprivation of the enemy. Thus, the total or partial embargo applied to North Korea, China, and North Vietnam certainly caused them inconvenience during the periods of hostilities and probably has affected adversely the total flow of supplies they received.

At the present time, however, this country's East-West relations still are afflicted by political mistrust and tension that might last for a long time. In such a situation, restrictions on trade almost certainly result in more loss than gain. In some cases their effect on security may actually be negative. By withholding important products or technology from countries such as the U.S.S.R. and China, we may encourage them to develop the needed technology and productive capacity, thus strengthening their capacity for future conflict.

Some observers who would accept the above arguments as valid hold to what might be called the "pariah" doctrine. They see advantage in labeling some countries as pariahs or outlaws to minimize their international influence. However, it is difficult to relate this argument to national security in view of the policy that the United States has been following. Although the Soviet Union has been considered more of a threat to the security of the United States than have other communist countries, Washington has recognized and dealt with the U.S.S.R. since 1933. The United States was its ally during the critical days of World War II, and in the years since the height of the Cold War has maintained a relatively favorable relationship with Moscow compared to that with Peking.

There remains the problem of determining what exports actually need to be restricted in the interest of U.S. national security. Apart from war material and equipment, we doubt that any goods should be on the restricted list—unless they would disclose the secrets of advanced technology important for military purposes. The export of technology itself presents a very troublesome issue. Technology involves a form of investment for which the payoff is special knowledge that provides a major key to increased productivity and the creation of new products. The problem is to identify the kind of technology which the owners are generally free to sell abroad but which should be withheld from communist countries because it is closely related to military capacity.

The fact that the transfer of a technology will strengthen the economy of a potential enemy is not necessarily a sufficient reason to deny the transfer. If a country can build better roads as a result of having the technology, it can indeed move troops more effectively. But this is a very minor aspect of the economic development that can be achieved through better roads. The risk that a potential enemy may thereby be made more dangerous is simply one of the risks that probably should be taken in an always uncertain world. The gain to us is a more open and less hostile relationship that could become the basis of a more peaceful world.

We recommend that the United States remove all restrictions on exports to communist countries with the exception of military equipment and the kind of advanced technology that would be particularly useful in producing such equipment. Except for such technologies as may be known only in the United States, we also recommend that the U.S. list of restricted goods and technologies be made identical with the COCOM list.*

EXPORT FINANCING

Credit terms are often a key element in making a sale, especially in a highly competitive market. Special U.S. restrictions on both government and private credit have impaired the ability of U.S. producers to compete effectively in selling nonrestricted goods to communist countries. The granting of foreign aid to communist countries is forbidden by statute, while a 1968 law prohibited the Export-Import Bank from extending credit, or participating in guarantees or insurance, in connection with a purchase destined to any communist country except Yugoslavia. The restriction could generally be waived by the President, though not in the case of countries furnishing assistance to a nation engaged in

---

*See Memorandum by MR. HERMAN L. WEISS, page 51.

armed conflict with the United States. In 1971, the 1968 law was modified to remove this limit on the President's discretionary authority, and late that year he waived the restriction for sales to Romania.

The restrictions on private credit that involve no government guarantees date back to 1934 legislation. This prohibited loans to nationals and corporations of countries whose governments were in default on debts owed to the U.S. government. Among the many countries in default were all the European communist countries except Bulgaria and Albania.[6] The failure of the U.S.S.R. to reach agreement on repayments to the United States for lend-lease shipments after World War II is also considered a default.[7] By the Attorney General's interpretation, private credits to finance commercial export sales of products or services are exempt from the prohibition regardless of the form the credits may take. The prohibition, however, continues to apply to other credits to these communist countries, and to purchases of their government bonds,[8] even though they are not the only countries still in default.

Restrictions on loans or credit sales to Eastern countries have sometimes been justified on the ground that the risk is greater than on credit granted to other countries. All experience since World War II indicates that the prospect of failure to meet contractual obligations has been no greater for communist countries than for many others. The present credit rating of communist countries is excellent.

It may be argued, however, that U.S. sales on credit to a communist country would increase that country's ability to provide foreign aid to third countries, possibly to the disadvantage of the United States. This argument clearly is valid when such foreign aid consists of convertible currencies or the goods that were bought on credit. Most communist foreign aid appears not to have been of these types, but rather to have taken the form of goods and services that could not otherwise

---

[6]/The statute was the Johnson Act of 1934. Later legislation exempted from the prohibition members of the IMF and the World Bank, of which organizations the communist countries are not members.*

[7]/New negotiations regarding payment for these lend-lease shipments have been held recently.

[8]/Since most long-term credit on sales of goods is guaranteed by the Export-Import Bank, which is still prohibited from making such guarantees for sales to communist countries except Romania, the effect of the Attorney General's opinions has been to facilitate short- and medium-term credits, but not long-term credits, until the 1971 legislation is implemented by Presidential order. Moreover, an Attorney General's opinion is not a sufficient defense against later criminal prosecution. Accordingly, the Johnson Act is thought to be a deterrent to some banks and exporters on even the short- and medium-term credits.

*See Memorandum by MR. HERMAN L. WEISS, page 51.

have been sold for convertible currency. In such cases, the connection between the U.S. credit sale to a communist country and the ability of that country to provide foreign aid concurrently would seem to be remote.

Moreover, in the case of long-term projects in communist countries financed in part by foreign credit, it may be expected that each dollar of loan or credit will require the communist country to sink a good deal more than one dollar's worth of its own assets into the project. By the time the loan is repaid the communist country should have increased its economic strength. But presumably the lender has also been benefited through receipt of interest payments and the return of principal.*

The granting of credit should operate both ways. In dealing with Eastern countries, we believe there should be reciprocity and symmetry in credit terms. Some Western industrial countries have granted credits to communist purchasers that are repayable over ten years or more, but the reverse does not appear to be the practice. No doubt this is due in part to the different character of the goods being sold, and in part to a practice of treating communist countries as if they were less developed countries entitled to long-term credits without giving any quid pro quo. Moreover, communist and market-oriented countries have differed in their views of the functions of trade. Both groups export for noneconomic reasons—for example, to encourage the friendship of less developed countries—and extend credit on such favorable terms that it amounts to a form of foreign aid.

In market-oriented countries, however, exports are sought not only as a means of financing imports but also because they add to plant utilization, employment, business profits, national income, and government revenues. To get this valued business for their nationals, Western governments compete in granting or guaranteeing credit. Such competition makes it difficult for the United States not to grant equally favorable credit terms.

The problem of credit competition is, of course, not limited to sales to communist countries, and solution of the problem for these countries is only one aspect of the larger problem. Avoidance of competitive subsidization of exports to communist countries and realization of a degree of credit reciprocity are obviously not objectives that any country can achieve by itself. A high degree of international cooperation and coordination will be required. A beginning in this direction was made before World War II in the so-called Berne Union Agreement,

*See Memorandum by MR. HERMAN L. WEISS, page 52.

30.

which is a gentlemen's agreement among creditors in Western countries designed to limit to five years the term of credit extended to foreign countries. Although the U.S. government was not a party to the agreement, the five-year limit has been adhered to in U.S. trade with communist countries, despite the fact that other countries have frequently granted or guaranteed credit for as long as ten to fifteen years.

In the latter sections of this chapter we discuss at greater length the need for international cooperative action in the granting of long-term credits. **Pending the achievement of adequate international cooperation in regulating credit térms, we recommend that U.S. policy on credit terms to communist countries be aligned with that of other Western industrial countries.***

RESTRICTIONS ON IMPORTS

Since World War II many U.S. tariff rates have been greatly reduced through executive agreements authorized by the Trade Agreements Act of 1934 and succeeding legislation. These agreements were negotiated in the GATT on a reciprocal basis and included the granting of most-favored-nation (MFN) treatment to all members of the GATT.[9] U.S. law, however, was changed to forbid granting MFN treatment to all communist countries except Poland and Yugoslavia.

Indeed, the special restrictions on imports into the United States from the Eastern state-trading countries have included embargoes on the exports of some of these countries and higher than MFN tariffs in the case of nearly all of them. Although under its rules members of the GATT are entitled to receive MFN treatment from all other members, U.S. law does not allow MFN treatment for Czechoslovakia. Nor does it allow its extension to Romania which has become a GATT member recently, although Congress has before it several pending bills that would authorize MFN treatment to Romania.

Imports also are restricted by quotas and embargoes. In 1971, as noted earlier, President Nixon lifted the embargo imposed on trade with China at the beginning of the Korean War. However, the embargo still stands for North Korea, North Vietnam, and Cuba. Other legislation

---

[9]/The spread between the negotiated rates and the statutory rates is in many cases very substantial, and in some cases the statutory rates are prohibitive of imports. Under an escape clause provision, the President can restore higher rates up to the statutory level, in which case other GATT members are authorized to impose compensatory tariff increases on imports of other products from the United States.

*See Memorandum by MR. HERMAN L. WEISS, page 52.

imposes embargoes on imports of certain products from communist countries, notably certain furs from the U.S.S.R. and China.[10]

It is doubtful whether in recent years U.S. import embargoes have had any significant impact on the ability of China, North Korea, or North Vietnam to buy what they needed. In any case, the complete embargo by the United States on purchases from these countries and from Cuba does not appear to have reduced their longer-run ability to meet their military requirements. Cuba has been able to export to other countries and has been financially assisted by the U.S.S.R., while North Korea and North Vietnam have been supplied by both the U.S.S.R. and China. During the 1950's China sold goods to and received aid from the U.S.S.R. Moreover, as that channel began to close at the end of the decade, China had many other markets open in which to earn foreign exchange. In short, the U.S. restrictions on imports appear to have been virtually irrelevant in terms of our national security.

In all probability, the differentially high U.S. tariffs on imports from communist countries have substantially reduced Eastern markets for exportable U.S. goods, since over the long run the communist countries can buy only to the extent that they can sell. An additional special factor is the emphasis placed by the communist countries on bilaterally balancing their trade where this is feasible.

In 1970 the U.S.S.R. and most of the Eastern European countries did in fact buy more from the United States than they sold to it. However, the small volume of the total trade at least indicates the limiting effects that U.S. import restrictions have on the volume of our exports to the East. If total U.S. trade with communist countries were to grow substantially, the pressures for bilateral balance would undoubtedly increase; otherwise the communist countries would be obliged to secure a greater amount of foreign currency in order to make payment to the United States.

For the reasons discussed above, this Committee would like to see an end to the discriminatorily high tariff rates on imports from the East. Still, we do not believe it would be desirable for the United States to remove them simply by unilateral action. The granting of MFN treatment should be used as leverage to secure from communist countries benefits equivalent to those that are assured from other countries by application of the GATT rules of fair competition and nondiscrimination.

---

[10]/The United States also has an agreement with the Organization of American States regarding Cuba which includes an embargo on imports, but otherwise the U.S. import restrictions are entirely unilateral in character.

To promote more satisfactory conditions of East-West trade at this time, the United States could itself propose agreements on a country-by-country basis with the U.S.S.R., the East European countries and China. In such trading agreements Washington might offer entrance to our market on a most-favored-nation basis, national treatment of communist business carried on in the United States, and perhaps also more generous credit terms. In exchange, the United States could seek agreement by the communist countries to purchase a defined enlarged volume of exports from the United States, to avoid dumping or other disruption of U.S. markets, to afford better treatment to U.S. businessmen, and not to discriminate economically against the United States. To assure that such an agreement would be properly implemented it would be practical to make the agreement for a relatively short period of time, with renewal contingent on mutual satisfaction with its operation.

We recommend that the President be authorized to grant most-favored-nation treatment on trade with communist countries provided that in return they extend compensatory benefits to the United States.

INVESTMENT
AND COPRODUCTION AGREEMENTS

The line between credit sales and investment is an uncertain one, since sales on extended credit terms are a form of long-term loan. This kind of "investment" in the East by Western firms is not uncommon and sometimes carries a Western government guarantee of repayment. However, investment in this form must be distinguished from direct business investment since it does not carry with it participation in management and a share of profits.

Over the past few years organizational adaptations have taken place in communist countries to meet the requirements of a modern technological society; as yet they do not include acceptance of direct foreign investment in the sense of equity ownership or the Western concept of profit. In some Eastern countries, however, there has been movement in this direction through arrangements for coproduction agreements. This term can cover many specific types of arrangement. In general, a coproduction agreement involves a long-term contract with an Eastern country under which a Western company agrees to provide capital, technology, and sometimes managerial services for a project in the Eastern country. Ordinarily the contract calls for repayment and a return on the investment in the form of product derived from the project, or possibly in a foreign currency. Agreements of this type have been made by Western firms in several East European countries and by Japan in the Soviet Union. In December 1971, Secretary of Commerce Stans reported that such agreements in the U.S.S.R. might be feasible for the United States. So far there is no evidence that China has accepted co-production agreements or is considering them.

The coproduction agreement is by no means a new invention, having been employed in the noncommunist world for many years. For the Eastern countries it reflects a desire to secure the assistance of foreign enterprises and represents progress toward acceptance of such agreements on terms attractive to foreign investors.

Investment transactions by U.S. nationals in Eastern countries are subject, of course, to U.S. regulations and restrictions applied to investment by American companies in almost all other foreign countries. Requirements for special U.S. licenses as well as restrictions on the transfer of advanced technology could act as a substantial deterrent to U.S. investment in certain industries in communist countries. Credit restrictions might also be applied to such investments. Otherwise, no special restraints are now imposed by the United States on investments in communist countries aside from the continuing prohibition on transactions with North Korea, North Vietnam, and Cuba. Nor does the United States place special restrictions on investments in the United States by agencies of communist governments.

Joint ventures in either direction are legally possible and have occasionally occurred. Investment in communist countries may arouse U.S. public opinion, however. In the past some American firms dependent on consumer acceptance at home have been dissuaded from undertaking projects in communist countries by expressions of public displeasure. Projects by American firms to produce manufactured goods in communist countries for sale in the United States would be particularly liable to criticism and possible adverse reactions, especially by the labor unions.

Like export credits, foreign investments made in communist countries, under coproduction arrangements or otherwise, are in competition with investments made by other industrial market countries. To the extent that the governments of these countries provide investment guarantees against expropriation or other political harassment, the United States must be prepared to follow suit. However, it should seek through multilateral agreements to impose reasonable limits to the terms of all such agreements.

34.

We recommend that, subject to limitations on the export of technology, the U.S. government place no obstacles in the way of U.S. companies entering into coproduction agreements in communist countries or otherwise investing there, except for obstacles that apply to foreign investment generally. We recommend also that the U.S. government seek multilateral agreements setting reasonable limits to the terms of government credits or investment guarantees for capital invested in communist countries, and that in the absence of such agreements it should be authorized to meet the competition when this would be in American national interests.*

NEED FOR INTERNATIONAL RULES

In determining the policy positions recommended in the preceding sections, an important consideration has been the policies of other industrial countries which are competitors of the United States in trade and investment. There are a number of respects in which we believe policies could be further improved if they were developed multilaterally in intergovernmental organizations. The United States has been a leader in promoting international trade among Western countries through intergovernmental organizations. Now it should try to obtain agreement on multilateral policies relating to trade with Eastern countries.**

Several problems in particular call for multilateral action:

1. There is clearly a need for the United States and other Western countries generally to encourage fair trading practices on the part of communist countries, especially since the GATT rules cannot be made fully applicable to them. A promise to buy more from GATT members on a multilateral basis, such as Poland made in applying for admission to GATT membership, may provide sufficient protection in the case of East European countries. However, other commitments should also be sought from the Soviet Union and China, specifically to avoid dumping or other disruption of Western markets, to afford better treatment to Western businessmen, and to avoid trade discrimination.

2. Effective arrangements for consultation and cooperation are needed among Western countries in their trade relations with the East to prevent them from taking discriminatory actions against each other.

3. The desire of Western countries to promote their export sales has led to competition in providing government credit and credit guar-

*See Memorandum by MR. PHILIP SPORN, page 52.
**See Memorandum by MR. G. BARRON MALLORY, page 53.

antees, often leading to unsound credit practices—for example, by providing financing terms for foreign sales which are more favorable than for the safest domestic sales. Wide differences exist among nations in the scope and terms of government programs to finance exports and to guarantee export credits. We believe these differences should be reduced through better international consultation and agreement, particularly with respect to exports to communist countries.

4. Similar competition should be avoided in the case of long-term loans and coproduction agreements in communist countries. International rules should be adopted to set standards for and limits to the terms of such agreements, especially covering government financing or insurance of the funds involved.

5. International consultations leading to the periodic revisions of the COCOM list have worked reasonably well, and the United States should support their continuation.

The need for a better system of international rules will become crucial in connection with each of the problems mentioned as the volume of trade and investment transactions increases between West and East. This need should be met before discriminatory practices become so embedded in national policies that they make achievement of international agreement extremely difficult.

We urge that the United States government renew and continue its efforts to secure international agreement on more adequate rules to protect the economic interests of each Western country against unfair governmental competitive practices on the part of both communist and noncommunist countries.

By their nature, multilateral agreements cannot be brought into being without agreement in different countries on what should be done. Sometimes this cannot be achieved at all. At best, it usually involves a long process of discussion and negotiation. We are pleased to state that several foreign counterpart organizations of CED, which have previously joined in cooperative efforts with this Committee, have cooperated in preparing the findings and recommendations contained in the joint statement that follows.

36.

MULTILATERAL POLICIES
FOR EAST-WEST
TRADE AND PAYMENTS

A Joint Statement prepared by
the Research and Policy Committee of CED
in association with

CEPES—Committee for Economic and Social Progress
(Germany)

CRC—Research and Study Center for Business Executives
(France)

Keizai Doyukai—Japan Committee for Economic Development

PEP—Political and Economic Planning (Britain)

SNS—Industrial Council for Social and Economic Studies
(Sweden)

*(The Chairmen and Members of the Executive groups of the above-mentioned
organizations are listed on pages 66-67.)*

■ This joint statement addresses the special difficulties that are retarding the development of trade and other economic relations between the market economies, which for convenience are called the "West," and the centrally planned, state-trading socialist economies, for convenience called the "East." It is addressed in particular to the possibilities of using multilateral negotiations and organizations to reduce these difficulties.

In addition to various political and ideological issues which have slowed the development of economic relations between East and West, a continuing major difficulty arises from differences between the two systems of production, trade, and prices. In the Western economies the structure of prices for transactions within each country is interrelated with the structure of external prices, which thus plays a key role in allocating production and trade. In the Eastern countries, however, the general pattern is for production and internal prices to be centrally planned, and not necessarily reflective of market forces, so that the economic, social, and political objectives of the government can be promoted. As a consequence, in these countries there is a separation of domestic prices from international market prices, and exchange rates are somewhat arbitrary. The supply of convertible foreign exchange in Eastern countries is partly dependent on planned resource allocation, which in many of these countries has resulted in an apparent shortage of foreign exchange and a failure, except to a limited extent, to use it to settle accounts with other Eastern countries.

Despite the basic differences between the economic systems of the East and West, we believe that trade and economic cooperation can increase more rapidly than it has in the past.

The trade of the industrialized Western countries with the Eastern countries is less than 4 per cent of total trade of the Western countries. This low ratio nevertheless represents a substantial volume. In 1971, the exports of OECD members to the Eastern countries stood at $8.2 billion, and imports at $7.8 billion.[1]

In the market economies, the individual firm has played the main role in trade expansion. Business initiatives have provided the major thrust in overcoming many of the problems of East-West trade. They continue to be the prime movers in developing East-West economic relations in new directions: for example, through cooperative agreements

---

[1]/Organization for Economic Cooperation and Development (OECD), *Statistics of Foreign Trade,* Series A (April 1972). Does not include trade between West Germany and East Germany.

(licensing, subcontracting, and coproduction agreements with some of the characteristics of investment) and through helping the Eastern exporters to market their goods in Western countries.

Because of the special nature of East-West trade, however, the role of governments is particularly important in creating the legal and administrative framework. As a result of the preference of state-trading countries for bilateral agreements, this framework has been largely the responsibility of national governments rather than of international organizations. Thus far this has been true of the members of the European Community (EC), but they have decided that authority in matters of commercial policy is to be fully transferred in 1973 from the member states to the enlarged Community. The intention of the Community is to negotiate Community agreements with each Eastern country.

Japan has had bilateral agreements with many Eastern countries either at the government-to-government level or at the nongovernmental level, and anticipates adding a few more in the course of current negotiations. The United States, for its part, is not well placed to lead the move to multilateral solutions until it has strengthened its trading position with the COMECON[2] group and China by entering into bilateral agreements with them. The Eastern countries continue to place the emphasis strongly on bilateral trading agreements, particularly among themselves but also with Western countries.

Multilateral institutions nevertheless do perform a significant role in East-West trading relations. Consultations on the subject among industrialized Western countries are carried on in the OECD by its members, and the restriction of exports of strategic importance is agreed to within the Coordinating Committee on Export Controls (COCOM). The Berne Union Agreement deals with credit terms. Some East European countries are members of the General Agreement on Tariffs and Trade (GATT), and most of the countries engaged in East-West trade are members of relevant United Nations bodies, in particular the United Nations Conference on Trade and Development (UNCTAD) and the various regional economic commissions.

In part, these institutions are dealing with problems which arise in trade between the market and state-trading economies but are not limited to this trade. Thus, difficulties in the regulation of credit terms

---

2/The Council for Mutual Economic Assistance is an economic organization of the centrally planned economies of Eastern Europe (Bulgaria, Czechoslovakia, East Germany, Hungary, Poland, Romania), the U.S.S.R., and the Mongolian People's Republic.

apply as much to trade with the less developed countries as to that with the state-trading countries. State enterprises are not peculiar to the Eastern countries but also exist in the Western countries, and Article XVII of the GATT provides in principle for the regulation of their trading activities. Nor have the state-trading countries been the main source of market disruption in the countries with market economies.

However, trade between countries of the two groups has many special features that call for special treatment in the multilateral bodies. Thus, state enterprises which operate in the context of a market economy, and often quite independently of the government, present a different problem for international trade than the trading monopolies of Eastern countries, which are subject to detailed government control according to a central plan. The identification and measurement of dumping is one thing where prices are determined in the market, but quite another where prices are centrally determined by the planners. A related difficult problem in East-West trade is the determination of appropriate prices of products derived from the East but resold in the West. The prevalence of bilateral balancing and bilateral agreements also presents particular problems for regulating trade and payments.

Economic reforms in Yugoslavia have introduced many of the elements of a market economy and thus have greatly reduced the special problems that Yugoslavia presents for international trade. The "new economic mechanism," introduced by the Hungarian government in January 1968, has reduced these problems with respect to Hungary also. But at present there is no indication that state-trading countries generally will make far-reaching reforms toward market-oriented systems for a long time to come.

Thus, the special features of East-West trading relations will remain. In the immediate future, at least, multilateral institutions will not generally perform a central role because of the emphasis on bilateral dealings. Yet multilateral agreements have already proved useful, whether reached in the United Nations Economic Commission for Europe (ECE) between the large majority of the countries involved in East-West trade, or in the GATT between certain state-trading countries and the majority of market economies. It is important to pursue vigorously the process of reaching multilateral agreement between Eastern and Western governments on the framework and procedures of trade.

The need for a better system of international rules will become more important as the volume of trade and other forms of industrial cooperation increases between market and state-trading countries. With an improved system of rules for East-West trade, it should be possible to protect firms against unfair practices in this trade as well as help to insure equity among countries in their trading relations.

The kind of economic organization best suited to serve the purpose of establishing appropriate international rules would be open to membership by both Eastern and Western countries and be global in scope. The Economic Commission for Europe has had the most experience in East-West economic relations. It is a regional organization of the United Nations and includes not only the Eastern and Western European countries, but also Canada and the United States. However, while the ECE thus brings together most of the countries involved in East-West trade it does not include either China or Japan. The United Nations Economic Commission for Asia and the Far East (ECAFE) might appear on the face of it to be the Asian counterpart of the ECE in East-West trading relations, now that China is a member of the United Nations. But the membership of the ECAFE is limited largely to countries in the geographical area implied by its name. Most of these are developing countries, and the majority of the industrialized countries outside of the region are not members.

The United Nations Conference on Trade and Development (UNCTAD) is a global organization including countries of both East and West, but its central concern is the trade of the less developed countries. The GATT also is a global organization but it has only a few Eastern members, not including the Soviet Union or China, and its central concern is trade among the market countries.[3]

There are three major problems of East-West trade which are not satisfactorily dealt with by the GATT. *First* is the difficulty of applying rules of nondiscrimination to imports of Eastern Europe from the West.

---

[3]/Four East European countries have now adhered to the GATT. Czechoslovakia has been a contracting party since the foundation of the GATT in 1947. Yugoslavia, Poland and Romania have acceded more recently. Discussions have been held with Hungary about its possible accession; and Bulgaria has had observer status since 1967.

Yugoslavia was able to establish to the satisfaction of the existing contracting parties that it applied the principles of the market economy sufficiently to qualify for inclusion under the normal GATT rules. For state-trading countries whose economies are organized mainly through central planners, however, this has not been found possible. Poland acceded, for instance, under a special agreement whereby the country undertook to increase its imports from each member of the GATT by a given percentage each year, in return for a binding by GATT members of most-favored-nation tariff treatment for Poland and some concessions relating to quantitative restrictions. Romania has recently acceded under a more flexible arrangement whereby the Romanians undertake to increase their imports by amounts corresponding to the growth of their exports. Such arrangements are believed to be useful to both sides.

Procedures have not yet been devised whereby nondiscriminatory behavior on the part of the state-trading countries can be established to the satisfaction of noncommunist exporting countries. *Second,* in the absence of common principles of price formation, the Western countries cannot adduce criteria other than market disruption to justify the application of dumping regulations to imports from the Eastern countries. And this, in addition to offering an inadequate rationale from the point of view of market economies, will sometimes appear arbitrary to the Eastern countries. *Third,* disruption can also be caused in third markets when the Western countries reexport products received from the East under coproduction arrangements or bilateral trading agreements. The disruption arises from the absence at present of an adequate test of the true cost of such products.

In view of the geographical and operational limitations of existing organizations, we recommend creation of a new global economic organization representative of the countries of both East and West in order to develop a new and comprehensive framework for resolving the problems of East-West trade. Discussions of course should continue in existing organizations on ways in which concepts of fair trading can be developed and eventually applied.

While institutions containing members from both East and West offer the most fruitful context for the growth of economic cooperation, the organizations containing only noncommunist countries also have significance. Thus, the discussions on East-West economic relations now carried on within the OECD are useful and should clearly continue.

The NATO[4] countries and Japan, as members of the COCOM, establish the list of commodities and technologies whose export to the Eastern countries is embargoed. Over the years this list has been reduced until it is focused mainly on items of substantial military importance. **The COCOM list should be revised periodically to ensure that it does not contain items other than processes and products of advanced technology that are important for military purposes.**

With respect to credit, the unofficial Berne Union Agreement of creditors, which was initiated in the 1930's, set a five-year limit to the terms of international credits. In recent years the Berne Union Agreement has been widely disregarded and the OECD is seeking to develop a system of more orderly competition in export credits. It has already concluded two intergovernmental agreements. One provides for ex-

---

4/North Atlantic Treaty Organization.

change of information and the other, in which most countries have joined, calls for prior consultation on credit terms. In addition the OECD is beginning to explore the possibility of more substantial agreements on credit terms for particular export sectors.

Credits to state-trading countries present a particular problem since transfers of finance and technology to most of these countries ordinarily cannot take the form of direct investment as they do elsewhere. The desire to facilitate East-West economic cooperation suggests that other types of long-term arrangements should be recognized as legitimate in any regulation of international credit or investment. **We recommend that in its negotiation of intergovernmental agreements on credit terms the OECD make provision for such special types of financial arrangements as may be needed to facilitate East-West economic cooperation.**

POSSIBLE STEPS
TOWARD MULTILATERAL PAYMENTS

Little progress has been made regarding the multilateral regulation of payments involved in trade between Eastern and Western countries. The Eastern countries have not applied to join the International Monetary Fund (IMF). Western countries have not been invited to participate in the limited multilateral clearing arrangements which have been established within the COMECON.

The development of multilateral payments arrangements has been inhibited by the system of bilateral trade and payments which the Eastern countries have generally pursued. Fully bilateral trade and payments between East and West, however, are not intrinsic to the system of central planning and state trading. There is nothing in this system which prevents an Eastern country from running a surplus with some market economies, offset by deficits with others. For example, the U.S.S.R. has habitually run a surplus in its trade with Britain, using its earnings to buy from other countries in the sterling area. Some Western governments, however, are still not prepared to accept deficits in their trade agreements with Eastern governments.

But if new international monetary arrangements enable governments to exercise greater freedom in their balance-of-payments policy, they may be ready to agree to depart from bilateral balancing in their trade with Eastern countries. If these countries did not wish to take advantage of this opportunity, then the trade would remain bilaterally balanced to the extent that it now is. But the example of trade between the U.S.S.R. and the sterling area shows that state-trading countries can in fact find it advantageous to balance deficits with some market economies by surpluses with others.

We suggest that the member governments of the OECD discuss how far they are willing to offer state-trading countries the opportunity to run trade surpluses with some Western countries to the extent that they are offset by deficits with others.

Greater difficulties would appear to stand in the way of multilateral trade in which an Eastern country balances a surplus with Western countries against a deficit with other Eastern countries. The state-trading countries seem reluctant to spend the convertible currencies they possess on imports from other centrally planned economies. Until these Eastern countries alter their policies toward each other, it will be hard to make progress with multilateral trade that has to be reflected in net transfers of convertible currencies between communist countries. The efforts to develop greater convertibility within the COMECON indicate that the countries of Eastern Europe wish to move in the direction of multilateral trade and payments within their own group. These efforts have been hampered by the difficulties inherent in central planning which thus far have prevented the establishment of viable exchange rates among the state-trading economies.

Looking to the longer run, if the U.S.S.R. and the countries of Eastern Europe succeed in achieving multilateral trade and payments within their own group, they may wish also to extend the process into their economic relations with the market economies. In such a case the Western countries may wish to cooperate with the Eastern countries in providing a multilateral source of international liquidity to strengthen their reserves of convertible currencies, whether by an arrangement between the IMF and COMECON's International Bank for Economic Cooperation or by other means.

We recommend that the countries which participate in the negotiations for reform of the international monetary system consider how they would cooperate with the Eastern countries in arranging a multilateral source of international liquidity should the Eastern countries indicate that they are prepared to move toward multilateral trade and payments in their dealings with the market economies.

MEMORANDA OF COMMENT,
RESERVATION,
OR DISSENT

Page 9—By MARVIN BOWER:

Many years ago, during a visit to the U.S., Premier Khrushchev boasted that the Soviets would "bury the West economically." A reminder of that boast is found in the Soviet applause and economic assistance given to the recent expropriation of the Iraq Petroleum Company.

I believe that the IBM slogan "World Peace Through World Trade" should apply to US/USSR relations. But since triumph over the West remains a goal of the Soviet Communist party, we should nevertheless keep Khrushchev's boast in mind as we resume trade relations with the Soviets.

Page 10—By STEWART S. CORT:

Although I am not in fundamental disagreement with the policy statement, I believe it does not deal adequately with the problems in expanding East-West trade, and therefore conveys an unduly optimistic impression of the benefits to be expected from the expansion of this trade.

45.

Page 11—By PHILIP SPORN:

This report has left me wondering why a group of hardheaded businessmen can so easily be beguiled by shallow philosophical shibboleths.

The opening statement says that special constraints should not be imposed on the functioning of international markets except as required by an overriding public interest. Yet it seems to me the report does not give sufficient consideration to the effects of the proposed policy on the strengthening or weakening of our political-economic organization.

It is stated, "willingness to trade is in itself a sign of amity that helps dissipate tensions. Through trade, moreover, new channels of communication are opened which help reduce the danger of either side misinterpreting the intentions of the other . . . Although improved communication and mutual understanding cannot be expected to solve fundamental conflicts of interest, they at least encourage a rational approach to negotiating a maximum area of agreement." These are glittering generalities and like all general statements contain elements of both truth and untruth.

In this paragraph it is stated, "The potential benefits of increasing East-West trade by removal of special restrictions are too promising to be neglected." This is a partial truth. Referring specifically to the USSR, the benefits certainly are not of immediate major significance and removal of restrictions does not have to be rushed; it is much more important that these potential benefits be carefully studied. It does not appear they have been in this report.

Page 14—By HERMAN L. WEISS:

I do not believe that the small U.S. share of Western trade with communist countries is primarily the result of special U.S. restrictions on trade with the East. Other factors including U.S. company inexperience in the East: adverse public opinion over the past two decades; inability (or unwillingness) to find Western markets for Eastern goods; all have contributed to the low level of trade. Perhaps one of the major reasons for the failure of U.S. trade with communist countries to keep pace with Western European nations is the lack of an effective bilateral trade agreement between the U.S. and Russia; in the absence of such arrangements communist enterprises have had to limit their trade with the U.S. to barter agreements or hard currency sales which have been difficult to achieve. U.S. business has been slow in developing trade with the East, caused by the absence of the necessary environment for bilateral trade, unfamiliarity of U.S. businessmen with procedures and an apparent high risk in doing business with communist enterprises; U.S. governmental restrictions should not be identified as the principal obstacle to normal trade with communist countries.

46.

*Page 14—*By STEWART S. CORT:

The policy statement refers to the differences between price and cost relationships in Eastern and Western countries. Yet it does not present any hard evidence on what the comparative advantages are between Eastern Europe and the United States. "Complementarity" between the United States and the Communist countries may be quite a different issue before rather than after "taking into account not only comparative advantages in production but also geographical location and costs of transportation."

*Page 15—*By STEWART S. CORT:

The obstacles (i.e., the objectives of the "other side") involved in negotiations for marketing of U.S. products in communist countries, and the distribution of Eastern products in the West (if payment is made in kind, as it often is) deserve more than passing reference. There should be an increasing body of information available on this subject, which would be of interest to readers of the policy statement.

*Page 16—*By GAYLORD FREEMAN:

It should be mentioned that some of these cooperative ventures might involve such large capital costs that they could not be financed entirely by private business firms.

*Page 16—*By STEWART S. CORT:

In this paragraph the policy statement raises the question of the profitability of the heavy investment and other commitments in Eastern countries. This subject should have been dealt with more fully, since there would appear to be some evidence to indicate that joint ventures in these countries are and will be much different—both as to longevity and rate of return—from those in other countries.

*Page 16—*By HERMAN L. WEISS:

The reference to the U.S. lack of competitiveness in consumer goods due, in part, to the matter of cost of production, is somewhat misleading. It is true that U.S. firms are particularly non-competitive in consumer electronics manufacturing. In many other product lines, however, U.S. manufacturers do have production costs equal to, or lower than, their European competitors; but due to the economic framework within which West European firms operate, including lower profit margins, tax advantages, and preferential treatment,

U.S. firms sometimes find themselves uncompetitive in price. Nevertheless, I agree that there will be little export trade in consumer products in the foreseeable future. However, the Soviets and others seem interested in licensing unique U.S. design and manufacturing know-how in some of the more technical consumer product lines. This may involve component sales.

Page 17—By GAYLORD FREEMAN:

The realization of two-way trade resulting from coproduction arrangements will depend not only on the continued reduction of U.S. restrictions on trade with the East but also on satisfactory financing.

Page 17—By PHILIP SPORN:

This talks about estimating the probable rate of growth of trade with communist countries including investment in coproduction arrangements. But the real question in my judgment is should we be prepared to enter into such trade and to make such capital investments.

Page 17—By HERMAN L. WEISS:

The increase in growth of U.S. trade with communist countries resulting from investment through coproduction arrangements will also depend to a large degree on the ability of U.S. firms to locate and develop Western markets for goods manufactured in the East.

Page 17—By PHILIP SPORN:

The USSR stands for the easing of international tension and for the expansion of mutually advantageous international trading. Let us examine the record:

(a) The record since Stalin does not bear this out. Khrushchev repressed freedom in Hungary, built the Berlin wall, emplaced offensive missiles in Cuba, and helped Cairo and Hanoi in military action against Israel and South Vietnam. Brezhnev invaded Czechoslovakia, continues to support Egypt in the Middle East, supplied the massive number of tanks and artillery for the recent invasion of South Vietnam across the demilitarized zone.

(b) How about economic aggression? To quote *The Wall Street Journal* editorial of June 6:

> The ink was hardly dry on the documents of friendly intentions signed in Moscow 11 days ago before Izvestia, the Soviet government newspaper, was declaring Iraq's expropriation of Western oil interests was a "great victory for the Arab peoples."

48.

To quote the editorial further:

> There has been rising concern that the Soviet Union is seeking to interpose itself between left-leaning Arab oil nations and these Western customer nations . . .

> . . . The Soviet role as political sponsor and oil broker for fractious regimes in the Middle East would pose a threat to nations which already have fundamental political conflicts with Russia; it can only increase the sense of conflict and undo the good feeling of the summit.

Petroleum is the vital source of energy of western Europe, whose welfare is indispensable to our own economic and political welfare. This Achilles' heel of western Europe presents to us the grave danger that Russia may at will close the fuel spigot on which this area's economic development depends.

(c) Business aggression: since the Russians do not believe in private business, the attitude of government business in Russian society toward private business in a society like ours is basically aggressive. In the recent business discussions they have been stipulating the terms on which they would do business with us. Mr. George W. Ball in *The New York Times* of May 21 says that they want credit of from eight to ten years with interest at 6%. A figure of 2% or 3% has also been mentioned. Now, why should we offer the Russians such terms when TVA, a top business owned by the Government of the United States, has to pay 7.5% interest on its AAA bonds?

Page 18—By PHILIP SPORN:

I wonder how authentic is the judgment that public opinion now appears to be supporting the relaxation of restrictions on trade with communist countries? Why should it? And may not organized labor, which has recently expressed opposition to increasing imports from communist countries, be closer to down-to-earth realities than this CED report? Let us ask three important questions:

First, in an interview in *The New York Times* of May 30, 1972, Mr. Mikhail I. Misnik, a deputy chairman of the State Planning Commission of the USSR, is quoted as saying, "the Soviet Union might be interested in building a large passenger-car plant for which the United States would supply the capital equipment. The Russians would be prepared to pay with finished cars that could be marketed by the Americans in, say, Western Europe." Why should labor—indeed, why should the country—be in favor of the idea? If we are going to build new automobile plants why not in the underdeveloped parts of the United States?

Second, what advantage do we gain by increasing imports from communist countries? Increased trade? Compare this bag of peanuts with the

49.

increased domestic trade we could have if we managed by industrial development of underdeveloped USA to bring up the level of income of its underprivileged inhabitants by $1,000 a year per family unit.

Third, labor knows that communism and the welfare of labor do not go together. Labor has watched communist countries' labor enslaved by the state and believes that communism is labor's sworn enemy. Why cannot American business, including CED, have the same clear vision?

Page 21—By HERMAN L. WEISS:

I disagree with the sense of this paragraph regarding the suitability of licensing, patents and know-how in the USSR. Licensing of patents and know-how on the basis of net sales billed can be difficult because of the fundamental difference in the communist pricing system, because of the difficulty in auditing results and because of the communist expectation of sharing know-how information obtained with other state enterprises. However, the licensing of patents and know-how on a fixed fee basis is not only feasible but well established. Legal protection for patents as such has not been tested but enforcement of international agreements appears to be functioning adequately. In spite of apprehension on the part of non-communist businessmen licensing agreements appear to be a profitable and practical means of trade.

Page 21—By PHILIP SPORN:

As to progress by the USSR in protection of industrial property, payment of commercial debts, and the belief that Russian performance in that regard is good: Let us take a look at the Soviet Union's World War II lend-lease debt to the United States.

This is a postwar incurred debt and originally amounted to $2.6 billion. The Soviets have never paid a cent's interest on it. Roughly 24 years have elapsed since the debt was incurred. If you charge against the original debt interest at the rate of 3% compounded annually the debt now amounts to $5.2 billion. We have been negotiating the repayment of that debt for years and according to the press our negotiators have offered to settle for $800 million. This is 15.5¢ on the dollar. The Russian offer is $300 million, less than 6¢ on the dollar. Is this a good record of paying their bills? To me it is a clear case of expropriation.

As to coproduction investments: Why should any prudent group of businessmen trust any deeply indoctrinated communist to resist the temptation to expropriate our capital investments in coproduction facilities? After all, if they did expropriate, what remedial action would be available to us?

Page 21—By STEWART S. CORT:

This subject is "a real can of worms", as any discussion with the Western Europeans involved in East-West trade will attest. How realistic is it to expect that real compensatory benefits will be extended? In view of the lack of information on the facts affecting comparative advantage, how does one determine whether such "quid pro quo's" are meaningful? What does the record show in various international commodities of the impact of Eastern countries on international trade?

Page 26—By STEWART S. CORT:

While I would not disagree with the proposition that trade may improve the underlying political climate, I do not think the statement sufficiently emphasizes the political risks in East-West trade today. No one knew until Mr. Nixon landed in Moscow whether the Summit talks would occur. The SALT agreements have not been approved as a whole or tested. The four Soviet interests in U.S. trade cited on page 26 may or may not be their real objectives in the long run. Only time will assess these political risks, but they do underlie East-West trade and should be emphasized in the statement.

Page 26—By HERMAN L. WEISS:

I believe foreign licensees should be included in this sentence, e.g.— "As a result of the U.S. controls, American business firms and their foreign subsidiaries and licensees. . . ."

Page 28—By HERMAN L. WEISS:

I believe that restrictions on exports should be limited to matters that affect security and that these export restrictions should not be used as a matter of political leverage. The U.S. Government should determine the nature and extent of the security limitations which are properly involved. A more clearcut definition of the restrictive list is needed and an explanation of how this list can be interpreted in regard to the export of goods and technical data including the direct product of technical data manufactured abroad.

Page 29—By HERMAN L. WEISS:

The Johnson-Debt Default Act of 1934, under which a U.S. financier who lends money in most communist nations could be sent to prison for 5 years, has not been abrogated, and should be formally recalled, through appropriate legislative procedure.

Page 30—By HERMAN L. WEISS:

The need for routine credit-worthiness information on industrial customers in the socialist economies should be noted. This should be some kind of Dun & Bradstreet credit and experience report on state enterprises and agencies in the Eastern bloc countries. Information available to U.S. businesses should identify the nature of the credit risks involved in transactions with each agency, the authority of each agency or enterprise to make long-term fiscal commitments and the enforceability of contract commitments by these agencies. Oftentimes American businessmen assume they are dealing with the Communist State in business negotiations. Whether or not this is in fact the case under Soviet law will have substantial impact on the suitability of contract terms and credit arrangements.

Page 31—By HERMAN L. WEISS, with which FLETCHER L. BYROM has asked to be associated:

The need to align U.S. policy on credit terms to communist countries, with that of other Western industrial countries, must be stressed in its *two* basic aspects: (1) Deferred-payment credit directly to specific transactions, and (2) Large-scale, long-term "project loans" for economic development. The conclusion statement (bold face) should be clarified to read—**"we recommend that U.S. restrictions on credit terms to communist countries be lifted to enable U.S. firms to be competitive in these markets. Export financing should be administered by the Export-Import Bank and credit terms made available should coincide with terms being offered elsewhere."**

Page 35—By PHILIP SPORN:

I believe this recommendation, as well as the earlier recommendations on pages 28, 31, and 33, go too far and are premature. It might be well for American business to listen to one of the most perceptive and experienced public servants as well as one of the wisest businessman we have had in the last several decades. In *Newsweek* of June 5, Mr. George W. Ball says:

If one focuses only on these developments it is easy to conclude that our two economic systems must progressively adjust their methods until they resemble one another—which should bring on the millennium.

Yet such a conclusion assumes too much. It assumes, contrary to experience, that the party ideologues, who maintain doctrinal purity with all the zeal of the Inquisition, will let the managers and technicians move toward a market mechanism, when each time such a drift has tentatively begun the party has stepped in to slow the process. . . .

Yet one cannot overlook the primacy of the party or the *persistence of an evangelical faith in the world revolution, and Russia's anointed mission to bring it about* (my italics). Nor, finally, dare one ignore those Soviet institutions, habits and attitudes that owe far more to the national character and experience than to communist teachings—the age-old Russian pattern of repression and furtiveness, cruelty and suspicion, that has deep roots in history.

Page 35—By G. BARRON MALLORY:

The United States has much to learn from other Western countries (through, for example, the Economic Commission for Europe) in view of our meager trade at the moment with the COMECON countries and paucity or lack of other arrangements with these countries. It seems to me that our national posture should be to foster an increase in trade with the Eastern countries and also the encouragement of credit accommodations, coproduction agreements and joint venture agreements. However, we should be willing to accept guidance and help from other Western countries which have made progress along these lines in the past.

There is obviously a necessity to work out more adequate rules to protect the interests of all of the Western countries against unfair practices not only on the communist side but also on the Western side. A move by the United States to substantially reduce embargoes on imports and restrictions on exports would help to encourage the Western nations to work out rules to prevent unfair competitive practices. Further, a move by the United States to offer most-favored-nation treatment to Eastern countries (in exchange for reciprocal concessions) would indicate our willingness and desire to ease and encourage trade between the East and the West.

TABLE 1A: EXPORTS TO EASTERN TRADING AREA[a] FROM WEST, 1938-1970

(millions of U.S. dollars, f.o.b.)

Exporter	1938	1948	1953	1958	1960	1963	1968	1970
U.S.A.	169.4	400.4	1.8	113.2	193.2	166.4	216.8	353.3
EEC, Total[b]	536.6	213.7	331.8	929.0	1,230.5	1,196.4	2,762.4	3,404.4
Belgium-Luxembourg	46.3	67.7	66.1	114.3	138.5	83.2	165.6	193.6
France	48.1	35.5	63.2	190.0	273.5	284.5	649.7	734.5
Germany	370.0	14.8	78.8	439.8	536.4	454.0	1,127.0	1,474.6
Italy	38.4	48.3	62.9	121.4	212.4	290.6	612.1	767.2
Netherlands	33.8	47.4	60.8	63.5	69.5	84.7	208.1	234.8
EFTA, Total[b]	284.7	613.9	551.6	901.8	1,035.7	1,209.1	1,812.4	2,286.4
Austria	n.a.	30.1	58.4	128.4	166.4	198.4	301.6	378.6
Finland	5.2	158.2	179.3	192.8	193.2	240.0	315.1	374.3
Sweden	32.0	101.4	69.4	97.5	123.5	137.9	246.8	361.3
Switzerland	34.4	70.2	60.6	75.3	69.5	67.9	160.6	232.1
United Kingdom	192.9	155.4	92.6	290.1	360.0	411.5	618.6	727.8
Other EFTA	20.2	98.6	91.3	117.7	123.1	153.4	169.7	212.3
Japan	91.0	8.3	4.5	73.5	65.7	241.7	581.4	1,044.7
Canada	9.3	53.6	.5	30.5	45.8	276.7	277.9	271.4
Other OECD	28.6	28.0	37.8	104.9	103.0	121.8	239.6	267.3
OECD, Total[b]	1,119.6	1,317.9	928.0	2,152.9	2,673.5	3,212.1	5,890.8	7,627.2
Total West[c]	1,416.0	1,960.0	1,270.0	3,130.0	4,240.0	5,435.0	8,775.0	11,580.0
Industrial Areas	1,235.0	1,485.0	945.0	2,270.0	3,025.0	3,760.0	6,525.0	8,450.0
Developing Areas	181.0	475.0	325.0	860.0	1,215.0	1,675.0	2,250.0	3,130.0

a/Trade with North Korea, North Vietnam, and Mongolia is not included before 1960.
b/Member countries of EEC as of 1958 and of EFTA as of 1970.
c/Total West includes countries other than OECD countries. Cuba is included in the developing...

TABLE 1B: IMPORTS OF WEST FROM EASTERN TRADING AREA[a], 1938-1970

(millions of U.S. dollars, c.i.f.[b])

Importer	1938	1948	1953	1958	1960	1963	1968	1970
U.S.A.	**121.9**	**236.4**	**46.0**	**63.7**	**79.2**	**80.9**	**198.2**	**225.8**
EEC, Total[c]	**654.7**	**303.5**	**320.7**	**802.9**	**1,144.7**	**1,470.0**	**2,353.2**	**3,060.0**
Belgium-Luxembourg	*53.4*	*80.7*	*47.4*	*62.6*	*85.4*	*122.3*	*163.9*	*189.4*
France	*59.9*	*75.4*	*51.3*	*185.2*	*177.4*	*272.0*	*472.9*	*535.4*
Germany	*419.4*	*20.0*	*99.5*	*343.7*	*472.1*	*494.0*	*850.9*	*1,199.5*
Italy	*64.5*	*47.8*	*54.0*	*116.7*	*291.1*	*445.3*	*705.0*	*893.4*
Netherlands	*57.5*	*79.6*	*68.5*	*94.7*	*118.8*	*136.2*	*205.8*	*242.0*
EFTA, Total[c]	**435.6**	**744.6**	**680.5**	**922.9**	**1,233.2**	**1,391.3**	**1,992.0**	**2,508.2**
Austria	*n.a.*	*56.6*	*60.2*	*118.1*	*164.2*	*205.0*	*251.9*	*345.5*
Finland	*15.8*	*92.8*	*182.3*	*187.1*	*260.0*	*253.2*	*331.2*	*431.3*
Sweden	*49.4*	*139.9*	*61.3*	*85.1*	*127.3*	*161.8*	*250.0*	*349.7*
Switzerland	*41.0*	*72.5*	*50.6*	*57.5*	*57.2*	*71.5*	*106.9*	*152.8*
United Kingdom	*288.0*	*243.0*	*234.9*	*337.7*	*459.1*	*533.2*	*810.6*	*955.9*
Other EFTA	*41.4*	*139.8*	*91.2*	*137.4*	*165.4*	*166.6*	*241.4*	*273.0*
Japan	48.9	27.4	37.7	79.3	112.9	255.0	836.6	886.8
Canada	5.7	8.9	5.9	15.9	19.2	23.6	92.6	82.8
Other OECD	57.4	35.4	35.7	121.0	118.0	182.6	308.3	316.8
OECD, Total[c]	**1,324.2**	**1,356.2**	**1,126.5**	**2,005.7**	**2,707.2**	**3,403.4**	**5,781.6**	**7,080.0**
Total West[d]	**2,095.0**	**1,970.0**	**1,610.0**	**3,315.0**	**4,080.0**	**6,000.0**	**9,760.0**	**12,230.0**
Industrial Areas	*1,760.0*	*1,530.0*	*1,200.0*	*2,180.0*	*2,820.0*	*3,530.0*	*6,220.0*	*7,750.0*
Developing Areas	*335.0*	*440.0*	*410.0*	*1,135.0*	*1,260.0*	*2,470.0*	*3,540.0*	*4,480.0*

a/Trade with North Korea, North Vietnam, and Mongolia is not included before 1960.
b/Except U.S.A. and Canada, whose imports are valued on f.o.b. basis.
c/Member countries of EEC, EFTA, and OECD as of 1970.
d/Figures are derived from data on exports from Eastern trading area.
n.a.: Not available.
Sources: United Nations, Direction of International Trade (for 1938 to 1958); and OECD, Statistics of Foreign Trade, Series A (for 1960 to 1970).

TABLE 2: INTERNATIONAL TRADE OF THE EAST RELATIVE TO WORLD TRADE, 1960 AND 1970

	Billions of dollars (f.o.b.)		Per cent Increase	Per cent of Eastern Trade		Per cent of World Trade	
	1960	1970	1960-70	1960	1970	1960	1970
TOTAL WORLD EXPORTS	128.32	312.50	143.5	—	—	100	100
Exports from Eastern Trading Area To:							
Industrial areas	2.82	7.75	174.8	18.8	23.6	2.2	2.5
Developing areas	1.26	4.48	255.6	8.4	13.7	1.0	1.4
Eastern trading area	10.83	19.79	82.7	72.1	60.3	8.4	6.3
TOTAL[a]	15.02	32.82	118.5	100.0	100.0	11.7	10.5
Exports to Eastern Trading Area From:							
Industrial areas	3.02	8.45	179.8	20.0	26.9	2.4	2.7
Developing areas	1.22	3.13	156.6	8.1	10.0	1.0	1.0
Eastern trading area	10.83	19.79	82.7	71.9	63.1	8.4	6.3
TOTAL	15.07	31.37	108.2	100.0	100.0	11.7	10.0

a/Total includes the following amounts of exports to unspecified destinations: 0.11 (billions of dollars) in 1960 and 0.80 (billions of dollars) in 1970.

Notes: Eastern Trading Area includes: in Eastern Europe: U.S.S.R., East Germany, Poland, Czechoslovakia, Hungary, Romania, Bulgaria, and Albania; and in Asia: Mainland China, North Korea, North Vietnam, and Mongolia. Cuba is not included in this area but in the Developing Areas. The Industrial Areas include Canada, United States, all of Europe not included in the Eastern Trading Area, Japan, Australia, New Zealand, and South Africa. The Developing or non-industrial areas include all other countries. In this table and those that follow, trade between East Germany and the Federal Republic of Germany is considered to be internal German trade and not trade between Industrial Areas and Eastern Trading Areas.

Source: GATT, International Trade 1970, Appendix Table E.

TABLE 3: INTERNATIONAL TRADE OF EASTERN TRADING AREA, 1960 AND 1970

(millions of U.S. dollars, f.o.b.)

Trade with	Exports from Eastern Trading Area				Exports to Eastern Trading Area			
	1960	1970	Increase	Per cent Increase	1960	1970	Increase	Per cent Increase
Industrial Areas, Total	**2,820**	**7,750**	**4,930**	**174.8**	**3,025**	**8,450**	**5,425**	**179.3**
North America	100	300	200	200.0	240	620	380	158.3
Western Europe	2,575	6,640	4,065	157.9	2,570	6,520	3,950	153.7
EEC	1,065	2,990	1,925	180.8	1,230	3,400	2,170	176.4
EFTA	1,185	2,480	1,295	109.3	1,030	2,270	1,240	120.4
Japan	110	750	640	581.8	75	1,040	965	1,286.7
Australia, New Zealand, South Africa, Total	35	60	25	71.4	140	270	130	92.9
Developing Areas, Total	**1,260**	**4,480**	**3,220**	**255.6**	**1,215**	**3,130**	**1,915**	**157.6**
Latin America	230	1,180	950	413.0	305	1,060	755	247.5
South and East Asia	610	1,380	770	126.2	470	960	490	104.3
Middle East in Asia	140	890	750	535.7	70	200	130	185.7
Africa	280	1,010	730	260.7	375	910	535	142.7
Eastern Trading Areas, Total	**10,830**	**19,790**	**8,960**	**82.7**	**10,830**	**19,790**	**8,960**	**82.7**
Unspecified	110	800	690	627.3				
World, Total	**15,020**	**32,820**	**17,800**	**118.5**	**15,070**	**31,370**	**16,300**	**108.2**

Note: Not all Western European Countries or developing countries are included in the totals. Trade between Mainland China, Mongolia, North Korea, and North Vietnam is not included in any of the trade figures.
Source: GATT, International Trade 1970, Appendix Table E.

TABLE 4: TRADE BY COMMODITY GROUPS BETWEEN WESTERN INDUSTRIAL AREAS[a] AND EASTERN TRADING AREAS, 1970

	Billions of dollars (f.o.b.)		Percentages	
	To Eastern Areas	From Eastern Areas	To Eastern Areas	From Eastern Areas
All Commodities	8.20	7.70	100.0	100.0
Primary Products, Total	1.52	4.01	18.5	52.1
Food	*0.92*	*1.44*	*11.2*	*18.7*
Raw materials	*0.42*	*1.06*	*5.1*	*13.8*
Ores and minerals	*0.09*	*0.36*	*1.1*	*4.7*
Fuels	*0.09*	*1.15*	*1.1*	*14.9*
Manufactures, Total	6.56	3.18	80.0	41.3
Non-ferrous metals	*0.33*	*0.36*	*4.0*	*4.7*
Iron and steel	*1.00*	*0.50*	*12.2*	*6.5*
Chemicals	*1.09*	*0.43*	*13.3*	*5.6*
Engineering products	*2.62*	*0.64*	*32.0*	*8.3*
Road motor vehicles	*0.18*	*0.08*	*2.2*	*1.0*
Textiles and clothing	*0.55*	*0.37*	*6.7*	*4.8*
Other manufactures	*0.79*	*0.80*	*9.6*	*10.4*
Not classified	0.12	0.51	1.5	6.6

a/ *Australia, New Zealand, and South Africa are not included.*
Note: Data are provisional.
Source: GATT, International Trade 1970, Table 10.

TABLE 5: 1969 EXPORTS AND IMPORTS OF OECD COUNTRIES TO MAINLAND CHINA BY COMMODITY GROUPS (thousands of U.S. dollars)

	EXPORTS, f.o.b.[a]					IMPORTS, c.i.f./f.o.b.[b]				
	Total OECD	Canada	Japan	EEC	EFTA	Total OECD	Canada	Japan	EEC	EFTA
TOTAL	969,259	113,239	390,800	297,894	166,399	691,854	25,366	234,538	268,016	159,359
Food and live animals	123,669	110,793	—	12,801	75	126,599	3,854	53,705	45,427	22,806
Beverages and tobacco[c]	150	—	1	72	41	6,546	—	99	5,781	666
Crude materials, except fuels	32,536	2,111	8,210	7,354	14,809	308,681	4,715	115,868	126,906	60,512
Mineral fuels, lubricants[c]	145	—	61	65	19	5,374	—	4,946	258	167
Animal and vegetable oils and fats	1,072	—	4	—	1,068	6,277	—	2,048	2,193	2,027
Chemicals	244,126	48	122,394	105,691	15,187	47,048	387	16,116	19,708	10,631
Manufactured goods, classified by materials	446,164	255	211,207	127,920	106,764	124,259	7,623	20,337	45,391	49,137
Machinery and transport equipment	98,260	28	44,376	35,356	18,485	1,349	86	221	623	259
Miscellaneous manufactured articles	21,656	4	4,437	7,383	9,832	63,462	8,595	19,511	21,349	13,074
Not classified	1,562	—	154	1,279	129	2,259	106	1,687	380	80

a/The United States reported 8 thousand dollars of exports to Mainland China.
b/The United States reported 29 thousand dollars of imports from Mainland China.
c/Includes exports to North Korea and North Vietnam.
Source: OECD, Statistics of Foreign Trade, Series C (1969).

CED Board of Trustees

See pages 5 and 6 for list of Research and Policy Committee and the Subcommittee members who are responsible for the conclusions in this particular study.

63.

65.

66.

67.

CED International Library

Increasingly close relationships are being developed with independent, nonpolitical research organizations in other countries. These organizations are composed of businessmen and scholars, have objectives similar to those of CED, and pursue them by similarly objective methods. In several cases, agreements for reciprocal distribution of publications have developed out of this cooperation. Thus, the publications of the following international research organizations can now be obtained in the United States from CED:

CEDA

Committee for Economic Development of Australia
343 Little Collins Street, Melbourne, Victoria

CEPES

Europäische Vereinigung für
Wirtschaftliche und Soziale Entwicklung
56 Friedrichstrasse, Dusseldorf, West Germany

PEP

Political and Economic Planning
12 Upper Belgrave Street,
London, SWIX 8BB, England

経済同友会

Keizai Doyukai
(Japan Committee for Economic Development)
Japan Industrial Club Bldg.
1 Marunouchi, Chiyoda-ku, Tokyo, Japan

CED

Council for Economic Development
Economic Development Foundation
P.O. Box 1896, Makati, Rizal, Philippines

CRC

Centre de Recherches et d'Etudes des Chefs d'Entreprise
31 Avenue Pierre 1er de Serbie, Paris (16eme), France

SNS

Studieförbundet Näringsliv och Samhälle
Sköldungagatan 2, 11427 Stockholm, Sweden

ESSCB

Ekonomik ve Sosyal Etüdler Konferans Heyeti
279/8 Cumhuriyet Cad. Adli Han
Harbiye, Istanbul, Turkey